UNTIL NOW

Kerri Link

FINN-PHYLLIS
PRESS

Published by Finn-Phyllis Press

Until Now / Kerri Link. — 1st ed.

ISBN 979-8-9905359-1-6 (paperback)
ISBN 979-8-9905359-2-3 (eBook)

Cover design by Debbie O'Byrne

To every person looking for light, healing, and truth.

And to my children, family, mentors, and support team.

My wish is that my words impact anyone seeking peace.

Foreword

I have had the honor of witnessing Kerri Link bloom—as a woman, as a writer, as an artist, and as a creator. I have watched with deep admiration as she's unleashed herself from a history that most wouldn't be able to unleash from. A history that didn't honor the holy force that she is and has always been.

Kerri is the exception to the rule. In every possible way. She is the model for overcoming. For grit, grace, and pioneering. She is the great gardener who has taken the deepest and darkest grief, and ground it all the way down to the very soil she planted herself in. The ground that she has nurtured tear by tear, therapy session by therapy session, growing the forever kind of roots. Roots that will hold her up, high and steady, as she takes on her big, bright, long, and beautiful life.

When I look at her, I am in awe. Complete and unwavering awe. I see her standing proudly in the middle of her garden that's growing wild and free all around her. Her face to the sun, with a look that says, "God, what else you got? I'm ready. Let's make it beautiful." In her true endearing and rebellious nature, she honors herself by honoring her experiences, her story, her life, in raw form. She doesn't soften them for us because she didn't experience them softly. She chooses what is rugged and true over what is easy and half-true, so that we may access our own truth without shutting down in shame.

And this is why her art matters so much. It's real. In a world that filters, she doesn't. Her art will change whoever encounters it because it offers hope and hope…and more hope—that it's never too late to live as the woman you ached for all the decades before now.

— Julie Harper | Founder, I AM HER

UNTIL NOW

Until now,
I told myself lies to survive, couldn't differentiate
reality from fantasy, refused to admit my marriage
was a lie or grieve the miscarriages, ignored my
instincts, focused on pleasing.

Until now,
I put my power on hold, settled for less and
underestimated myself, accepted disrespect,
refused to see my value, and felt the need to
defend myself.

Until now,
I didn't see the possibilities in life, that endings
mean new beginnings, that my mind can be a
beautiful place, that my essence will guide me, that
I possess tools to survive, and that I can walk hand
in hand with trauma.

Until now,
I didn't know if I would tell my story, if I could
create space for passion and magic, if I could allow
myself more than mere survival, if I could embrace

my younger self and convince her that God indeed
has a plan.

I thought disassociation and a life of make-believe
would keep me safe from my grim reality.

For years, a scared little girl followed me, and I am
finally learning how to reconnect to her,
to myself.

Until now,
I hadn't let her in. I was that little girl who
suffered, but I have grown into a powerful
survivor with beautiful scars that still need work
and gentle healing.

I am grateful to that little girl, my younger self, for
her strength and will to survive.

Because of her, I am here, I am worthy, and I am
changing my life's narrative with optimism,
acceptance, self-love, self-respect, and grace.

Fireflies

The magic that surrounds fireflies
transports me back to my childhood fantasies.

They travel through the air,
gliding through the dark,
through the trees.

Now you see me,
now you don't.

As I watch their sparkling fire come and go,
I want to live in the fantasy.

A quick getaway.
An escape,
absent of myself.

Pulling off the amazing disappearing act
as they glide into the magical night air,
I am reminded of their God-given magic.

Shirley's Open Door

Red hair and sparkling blue eyes,
having you in my life made me wise.

Your contagious laugh in the distance,
listening to loons on French Lake.
I'd go back to those days in an instant.

We drove, observing
white trilliums in Wildwood.

I was one of the lucky ones
who experienced a storybook childhood.

Everett, Shirley, Charles, Darla, and Sandra.
Now I only have photographs.
(Thank God for cameras.)

I will remember all you taught me
by caring for others in need.

You were a true earthly angel.
Your purpose on earth achieved.

You're a Know-It-All

People call themselves know-it-alls.
I never knew they were.
I never saw them that way.
I simply thought they knew everything.

Breaking Rules

Always wanting to color outside the lines.

Never wanting to be told I can't.

I will continue to follow most rules.

But if I'm honest, I like breaking them too.

Why Did You Choose Me?

Snow falling from the sky in late 1979,
Christmas trees lit up in every color,
nutcrackers, angels, and snow globes.
Beautiful jewelry sparkling in the windows,
store shelves full of Christmas ideas.
Cheerful people everywhere,
tinsel and glitter.
What a happy and joyous season.

Then I was chosen
to be taken
out of Christmas joy.
Dragged into darkness,
screaming for help.
What will become of me?
Will I become bones scattered
throughout the town?

Why have I been chosen?
If not me, it would have been someone else.
It was my turn to bleed.
It was my fate.

I could have died and been but a memory,

but I didn't die. I lived.

I got away; I survived.

God chose me as an example.

Be

I don't write for the abuser.
I write for the abused.
To remind you of who you are.
Who you were meant to be.

Detached From the Girl in the Hay

How am I separate from you, myself?
Are you not me, am I not you?

I can see you, but I can't feel anything.

Forty-five years have gone by.
I have suffered without your gifts all these years.

I am learning how to live in the joy,
remembering the love you brought to so many.

Children bring excitement and mystery to our
world, curious and happy.

Until the world teaches them not to be.

Keeping It Together

Dreaming keeps me awake at night.

One day all my words will be on paper.

Then I will be able to sleep again.

I won't let you shatter my dreams.

Greetings From the Garden

The bruises rest within me now.
They are nothing but a painful memory.

A reminder that someone wanted to cut me.
Cut me into pieces after bruising my body.

Burying pieces of me deep within the ground.
My place to rest was in the garden, they told me.

But you can't see me, Mom. You won't know I'm
there as you're drinking your coffee, looking at the
hydrangeas.

I am here, Mom, in the garden. Please don't cry.
I am in every flower looking toward sunlight.

Then I realize, I am alive, only with bruises.
They weren't able to follow through.

I see the lovely garden I was to be buried in.
Kidnapped, then raped, but I escaped.

UNTIL NOW

I am home.

I run to you, Mom; you are my safety.

And I am free, free to live my life.

Sitting by the window, looking at the garden

with you.

Living in Grief at Thirteen

My 13-year-old self saved me
from the monsters.

I viewed you as weak
as you were pushed
into the backseat
of an old car.

But you weren't.
You got away
as they slowed down
at a stop sign.

You were a brave soul,
and you need to know
that I am thankful to you
for being so strong.
Forgive me
for leaving you there
in the hay with blood.
I watched you die.

UNTIL NOW

Now I know that

you saved us, and

you are the hero, you chose life.

Monsters Live Everywhere

Am I trash or debris?

Why would someone rape me?

At thirteen years old.

Was it for the sex?

Or was it to dominate and control?

It happened, but I was able to disconnect.

I'm thankful for the years I was able to get by.

Time taught me I am strong and able to survive.

We Will Conquer Evil Together

For a short time
evil entered into
a child so pure
and managed to steal her security.
Let me hold your hand, dear child.
You did nothing to bring this sludge
into your life, your space.
You will always remain beautiful,
so full of life,
a child of God.
You didn't deserve to be raped.
None of us deserves evil.
Evil chooses to knock at our door
at different times in our lives
without our control.
Then we wake up,
years later,
needing to take it day by day,
sharing these important gifts
we have learned along the way.

Making Progress

I'm learning
to erase
all that you are.
But I won't forget.
So I can also learn to live again.

Not the Police

I was fragile after my abduction.
Always felt I had to protect myself.

Nobody protected little me, young me.

The policeman said I deserved to get kidnapped.
It was my fault for what I was wearing.

Dear God, protect the innocent.

What Is Freedom?

No longer in the darkness
will I allow you to grieve.
You wish for sunlight on your face,
dream of the ocean,
have a burning desire for life,
yearn to climb mountain after mountain.
Then I hear a voice I do not remember,
realizing it is my own.
I look back into those eyes and remind her:
You are safe now, and I love you.
You are home.
You are free from the pain you endured.
It is time to come and be one.
I am also ready to move on,
but with you.
Freedom has never looked so inviting.
Freedom from violence.
Free to make peace with the past.
Free to love my younger self.
Free to forgive my abusers.

Going to the Other Side

What is it like on the other side
of trauma?
A place where
we don't have to live in survival mode.
There is another world,
another way of living,
soaring high above trauma.
No longer in numbness,
not in death.
In total aliveness.

Never have I been so proud
as I am today of myself.
I have chosen to go forward.
Time makes it easier to crawl away,
to find your way out of the unknown.
to become open
to discovering new ground
that will elevate you toward freedom.

I'm Still Here

Do you ever wonder if I'm alive?
Did you think about getting caught?
Did it keep you awake at night?
Did you have nightmares of living in prison?
Did you ever regret kidnapping me?
Do you have a family?
Do they know what you did to me?
Did you try to find me over the years?

I still have nightmares of you finding me.
Do you remember talking about
cutting me into pieces?
Saying my disappearance would be a mystery?
I wanted to die for many years.
Life has been a struggle.
And until now, I didn't see myself as special.
But I am special.

You thought you had it all figured out,
then I destroyed your plan and got away.

I have found freedom.
Freedom in angels here on earth.

Freedom Is on the Other Side

Where I once felt safe,

every shadow or movement

had me living in a cage.

I was no longer living a normal life.

Any secure feeling had vanished,

my inner peace gone,

maybe forever.

Unable to walk down a street

without looking behind me.

Everything changed.

Mirrors, clothes, make-up, food,

authority figures, men, strangers.

Just as they wore masks,

I, too, would spend years wearing my own.

Baby, It Ain't Over Til It's Over

How long do victims suffer when they
continue to hear it was their fault?
Learning to hate themselves,
turn away from themselves,
place the blame on themselves.
How long does it take
to forgive someone who raped you?
Can you forgive those who failed to protect you?
I am choosing to forgive those who wronged me.
I've suffered long enough; it is time to move on.
I will no longer allow you to hold me down
like the rapists.
I was never at fault.
I free you all from the prison in my mind,
because UNTIL NOW, I believed you.

I Release You

Being taken
from a quiet little town,
I suffered abuse and injustice,
hands down,
from my abductors, the police,
teachers, doctors, peers.
I share my story to help you forgive,
let go, dry your tears.
Setting myself free
from years of torment,
no longer will I suffer
from the pain and judgment.

What Is Eating You?

I don't want it in me.
I won't put it in my mouth.
Going down my throat,
it must come out.
Why are they hurting me?
Why do they want to kill me?
Everyone questioning why I won't eat
when I would rather die than put food into my
body.
They want to know what is eating me,
but I can't connect, I don't understand.
They want to talk about when I was abducted
as I slowly try to kill myself.
It will be a slow death,
one where my organs begin to fail me,
my teeth crumble,
a death I deserve,
because I am nobody, I am nothing.
I am dead inside.
How do I find the strength to move on?
Will I decide to choose me and live life
instead of existing in this excruciating pain?

Swallowing Life Whole

We keep swallowing what people tell us.
Generations of women being the martyrs.

You're not an artist, give that up.
You're not thin enough, stop eating.
You can't write, do something else.
You need more makeup, less makeup.
Your hair is too long, too dark.
You will never amount to what I want for you.
Maybe I should take care of your children.
They will behave better with me.

I can't swallow anymore.
Can't I live the way I want to?
Dress the way I want to?
Parent the way I want to?
I don't want to fit into your mold.
I want to create my own definition of myself.
I am a good role model for my children,
but not because of you.
I don't want to bury my ambitions like you have.
It's okay to have dreams and desires.

Why should I settle for less?

I will no longer abandon myself.

I will not digest your idea of who I am.

I will no longer swallow

what society expects of me.

Comfortably Numb

I eat everything imaginable.

I learn a destructive pattern.

Bulimia becomes all I think about.

I hate food inside my body.

I hate my body.

I don't want to eat.

I learn that anorexia feels better.

I don't want to listen to the voice.

Why does my brain always talk?

It is perhaps the cruelest voice I know.

The doctor prescribes anti-depression drugs.

They keep the voice at bay.

They are not a cure; they keep me numb.

Why do doctors keep us numb?

Next they prescribe anti-anxiety drugs.

They keep me from crawling out of my skin.

I continue to drink alcohol mixed with drugs,

which forces me to black out,

the most toxic yet desirable combination.

It's as if I'm not alive anyway.

A slow death.

At some point, I look at my children.

I am not connecting with anyone,

but I am getting through the days.

Help me be okay with the pain, God,

so I can move on and live.

I am tired of wanting to die.

Skin and Bones

There is just silence.

Nothingness.

Bones.

Where are the words?

Grieving sometimes brings a loss of words.

There is only numbness,

flesh.

Gravity pulling at your organs.

Tugging so painfully toward the ground,

leaving no room to feel.

I don't want to express nothingness,

the emptiness.

But grieving is an individual experience.

It won't last forever.

I am not weak for staying here a while.

I can't help it if you can't understand.

I've been lost for years.

Starving.

I'm clawing my way back,

and I will rise from this stronger.

In the Air We Breathe

Until now, I haven't felt safe.

Seems to be a recurring theme in life.

I need to remain open,

grow, breathe.

I don't want to be in the ground

unless I am a lotus flower.

I don't want to be in the ocean unless I can float.

In an airplane, landing is the only way out.

Sometimes you're in the sky for hours.

I can't breathe if I can't open the window.

I can't be in a hotel room

without having the window open.

I slowly begin to suffocate

at the mere thought of no air.

How do you rest in a coffin

if you can't feel the sun?

Or breathe the air?

How do you sleep in a basement?

I can't breathe there.

I can't wear a Cartier bracelet

because they don't come off.

Why would you wear something

that won't come off?

I guess tattoos don't come off.

My tattoos are of God and my children,

but I can't scrub them off.

Why do we do anything permanent?

Once you're pregnant,

you're pregnant.

For nine months.

You can't go back.

Don't put food in your mouth.

Once you swallow, you can't take it back.

But how do you know what will bring anxiety

unless you live your life?

What is the anxiety from?

It's about not having control

over what happens to me.

I allow it to control me in other ways.

Through fear, anxiety, and food.

I want to be free

from being held down.

I want control of my body.

I don't want to inhabit the hell in my mind.

I am learning to free myself of the constant panic.

Trauma no longer holding me hostage.

KERRI LINK

Heads Up, Heaven

My heart bled when yours stopped.
I know it wasn't meant to be,
but now I need to set you all free.
My life had to go on,
but not without the memory of you.

Miscarriages Along the Way

I have not dealt with the loss of you.
I was so focused on producing life
that I didn't have time to grieve for you.
Having a dream ripped away,
new life that won't see the light of day
is devastating.
Carrying you and then
learning to carry the grief
has been heavy.
I need to transfer the pain,
allow it to fade away
so I will be able to weave the memory
of each of you within me
and begin to forgive myself one day.

How Many Times Will I Say Goodbye?

I hate the heartbeat game.
Are you still there, child of mine?
Will your heart continue to beat?
The anxiety seems to take control
like never before.
I slowly lose my mind,
day after day, week after week,
wondering if you will stay or go.
Wondering if your heart will continue beating.
Today is Mother's Day.
Twins growing inside me for four months
decided to leave me,
leave my body, leave me in pain.
Today was meant for celebration.
Instead, my mother chooses to lie on the floor,
holding me, our hearts beating together.
I'm grateful for this moment in life together.
It is a celebration of those of us who remain alive.
Goodbye, my sweet babies.
Goodbye.

My Five

I had my children
in my twenties, thirties, forties.

Every decade, continuing to add more love
to my beautiful story.

All five are creating
unique ways of blazing their own paths.

It is because of my *Fabulous Five*
that I continue to reach for more,
and climb to higher heights.

Was I the Happy Homemaker?

I was the happy homemaker,

living in isolation in a town of 527.

My occupation was getting pregnant,

and I wasn't having any luck.

Visits to specialists in artificial insemination

led to failed attempts that came with

crippling pain and cramps.

Bursting cysts and endometriosis

wrapping around my uterus.

In vitro became the next self-sabotage.

Injecting myself daily with five needles,

not wanting the world to know I was the failure.

The doctor made sure we knew

sperm count wasn't the issue.

Traveling hours to appointments to measure

my malfunctioning ovaries and uterus,

numerous egg counts that wouldn't amount to

many.

Would they even be healthy enough to fertilize?

What a humiliating and devastating time.

I was always alone,

miscarriage after miscarriage.

But you're going to keep going.
I want a bigger family.
It would be selfish of you to keep me
from having more children.

I miscarried in other states
and even other countries.
Two, three, four months along,
I was the only one counting.
How much more could a woman take?
With two children at home who needed their
mom,
I was nothing more than a means
to give him children.
I began unraveling inside
when the doctor said he was done.
He couldn't see me go through
any more miscarriages.
He had never known anyone capable
of enduring so much loss.
All the drugs in my body,
all the disappointment and grief,
all without the support of a husband.
I was exhausted and heartbroken,

but new challenges awaited.

Ones with surrogates, then egg donors.

Dr. Seuss had it right: "Oh the places you'll go."

Wish he would have mentioned the places to avoid.

The Magic of 5

My first daughter came out of the fire,
turning me into a warrior of strength.
My second daughter was born out of love,
sadly a love that didn't last,
but she taught me to love unconditionally.
Many miscarriages followed over the years.
Then, six embryos were placed in my uterus, and
my third daughter held on and made an
appearance,
teaching me to never give up on life.
The love I had left deep within me
brought me my sweet babies four and five,
twin boys who blessed our family.
I am so grateful for my children and to be alive.

You Came Out of the Fire, Sweet Kaila

We were blessed to live in the hot desert.
The pool made the heat enjoyable.
We lived our lives without fear.
You were only three years old.

We found freedom, a new life
in that one-bedroom apartment
and hiking up Camelback Mountain.

Over the years, we created many
wonderful memories to reflect on.
Some of the years were painful,
but we found ways to escape the flames.

My love for you will always be special.
I've watched you take the good from our earlier
years
and create a warm, beautiful life.

Please forgive me for the mistakes I made.
I never would have dragged you into hell
intentionally.

I'm a Mother And?

Am I being a good mom
if I conceal my dreams and my feelings?
Until now, I did just that.
I am now creating my own version
of what works for me and my children.
I won't abandon myself another minute.
I am a mother with years
of experience and education, and
I choose to mirror behaviors
that show I trust myself
as I live the remaining story of my life.
I can't continue going forward,
my children as my only priority.
I have tapped into the larger picture
that will pave the way to their freedom too.
We can be amazing parents,
while still living out our other ambitions,
recognizing that the world can be painful
but also magnificent.

Forever My Five

You are the glitter and all that shines in my world.

Yesterday, today, and tomorrow,

loving you is the greatest force in the world.

I can't imagine a greater love

than the one I share with each of you,

and the one you share with each other.

A Forever Love

There you were,
on the stage
shining bright.
So proud,
looking at us
with your big beautiful
brown eyes.
They walked in, and
you stopped singing,
turned white,
began fidgeting.
The concert came to an end, and
you were full of anxiety,
tears rolled down your cheeks.
Everyone knew you were struggling.
I'm so sorry that your story
with your grandparents came to an end.
The teacher held your little hand,
and I ran to you and picked you up.
I won't let anyone come near you.
You are of my soul.
I will always protect you.

You Chose to Shine

You were one of six on a journey.

You, unlike the others, chose to shine.

You held on for a chance at life.

You were blessed with a unique design.

You have become the hero in your story.

You are a gift, and we will forever align.

Strength in Scars, Keira Lee

You learned firsthand
what it was like to be bullied
by peers and adults.
Harassed on social media
as well as in person.
For having your nose bitten off
while being attacked by a dog.
You took the bandages off
and showed the world
that you were okay.
Even though your scars run deep,
they can't destroy you.
Instead, we learned lessons.
We learned that you are a bright light
and your beautiful soul will help others.
I am so proud because
you continue to trust your voice.
Being loyal to yourself takes strength.
Your scars will take time to heal.
But you have become a role model to others
and will continue to shine.

Forever With Me

Oh my little princess, Koko Chanella Bella.

How you became the key to my soul,

the joy of my heart.

You were one of the most important parts of my

life.

For 15.5 years, you raised kids with me,

kissed my tears away during a terrible divorce,

always by my side,

bringing joy to everyone who met you.

I am grateful that I was the one,

the one blessed to be with you,

to share my life with a puppy like you.

You kept my depression and anxiety at bay

so I could be a mother to five children.

You kept me alive during those years, precious girl.

Thank you for loving me.

Until we meet again, you are the wind

that makes the chimes sing.

UNTIL NOW

Kenia Adaline

Strong from the moment I felt your first kick,
and now you're off to conquer
a crazy world in politics.

You wear camouflage with a tiara,
have always known who you are,
and today it is even clearer.

Never doubt how much I adore you
and have loved every minute of my life with you,
it's true.

You were and forever will be
my baby conceived in love.

For your little brown eyes I will always
give thanks to God above.

Twins

Emerging from my soul,

you began to grow.

Manifesting

into the baby boys of my heart.

I knew from the very start,

never could we part.

My love for you will never end.

It's so clear,

I adore you more every year.

Connecting with you will always be key,

my baby boys you will always be.

Jayger Earl

Jayger, when I look at you

I see me.

You are complicated

yet gentle.

Sharp

yet soft.

Beyond your years

yet still such a boy.

For years I have tried putting a finger

on how to describe you.

You make me recognize

that there are good men in this world.

And when I am gone from this place,

you will make good choices.

I love that you push me to be better,

do better.

You are honest with me,

even when it hurts.

Just know that there will never

be a love in this world

like the one I feel for you.

Not ever.

I adore you with my entire soul,

and thank God for the gift

He gave me all those years ago.

UNTIL NOW

Jaxson Wilfred

Behind that smile
is a young man,
changing and growing into
someone I
continue to be proud of.
You are thoughtful,
sensitive and bright,
charming and witty.
You make life so special.
I will squeeze your hand
three times
in my mind
for the remainder of my life.
I am so grateful
not to have to live life
without you.
Thank you for
showing me love.
I will choose you.
I have always chosen you.
I will always love you,
now and forever.

Undecorated Doors

The Fourth of July was a magical time of year.
Fireworks, cooking out,
time on the lake with friends.
Water skiing, swimming, and tubing behind boats,
powerful boats with speed.
You were seven.
Water splashing in your face, you couldn't see.
How were you to know what would occur?
Then your body hit the sharpest part of the
pontoon,
splitting your head wide open,
your skull thrusting its way into your brain
before making its way through your clavicle.
You were in the water,
bleeding to death, your head wide open,
unaware of what was truly happening.
Life-flighted to Minneapolis with prayers.
How would you survive?
How would I survive without you?
God chose life, and you made it through surgery.
Priests and social workers were able to leave,
and eventually I walked you around the hallway

in a wheelchair.

You wondered why your door wasn't decorated

like so many doors on the floor.

It was because we knew you were going to live.

That day, we learned an important lesson together.

That the children behind decorated doors

weren't going home.

And God gave us a gift that day.

It wasn't your time to leave.

You were going home.

Your door remains undecorated.

What's Next?

You are all old enough to run toward
what you desire.
I am now seeing a light ahead,
calling me to venture out,
to search for what is calling me by name.
A voice that has been getting louder and louder,
echoing through the mountains between me and
new experiences.
Places to live, people to meet,
allowing my creative side to come to life.
I have never, in all these years, allowed myself
to believe I could be creative.
And I will forever listen to the voice inside me,
the voice that is driving me back to life.

Fingerprints on My Window

I see your little handprints
on my window.
I see where you licked the cold glass
as the sun shines through it.
Even though you live miles away,
my dear little Charlotte remains.
You have left your mark.
And as you grow, your hand will reach
higher and higher on the glass.
Maybe you will kiss the glass.
Maybe leave a nose mark.
Just as the generations before,
it comes full circle.

A Piece of Me

A piece of me
remained elsewhere
in the universe.
My heart became cold,
a gaping hole.
I wanted love, so did you.
You needed light, so did I.
We needed each other.

Words of a Father

Thank you, Dad, for knowing how
to communicate with me.
It wasn't easy, but we managed through life,
and I received a degree.
There were highs and there were lows,
but through it all our love continued to grow.
Thank you for the years you gave to my family,
memories we will always look back on happily.

We Were Both Killing Ourselves

Friends helping each other

through the battle of life.

Who will die first?

The one with a cig hanging out of his mouth?

Or the one who didn't eat?

Who will win the battle?

I'm glad you quit smoking.

I guess you win.

UNTIL NOW

MJL

When remembering life before and now,
you need to know you gave everything,
welcoming us when nobody else would.
We figured it out and life was amazing.
We created wonderful memories,
but he wanted you to erase your past
so that he could conquer the world.
And it wasn't fair to ask that of you.

You will always mean the world to me,
and I am sorry for the pain that
continues to linger all these years later.

You have taught all of us that we can move on.
We can move on and love each other.
It will never be what it should be,
but maybe in time it will be better.

I want you to know
that I will always love you,
and that I am grateful.
Grateful that there is a you and a me.

A Page Out of Your Book

I took a page out of your book
so I could write my story by the flowing brook.

I found I loved poetry
and you recognized my glory.

So I gave the page back and you made a toast
that made me realize I loved you the most.

Without your support and unwavering love,
I would be a star that doesn't twinkle from above.

You kept me on my journey to love myself again.
I have found my shimmering northern star,
Amen.

UNTIL NOW

My Dearest KB

A friendship that ebbs and flows
through an interesting lifetime of highs and lows.

With amazing kids, marriages, and careers
changing, to divorce, death, and lives rearranging.

You listen to my crazy chapters of the moment,
regardless of how insane, never holding judgment.

You are as beautiful as you are bright,
wherever you go, you carry a brilliant light.

Thank you for being my dearest friend indeed,
an expiration date between us there will never be.

Love you.

KERRI LINK

LA Through Kal's Eyes

Our time together was truly an unbelievable gift.
Our shared love of music
helped me make a transformational shift.
The Forum, Greek Theater, the Hollywood Bowl
would become important memories of my soul.
Seeing LA with love and persistence
was one of the best seasons of my existence.
You helped me see the good in a sea of monsters
and taught me that good always conquers.
Two lonely souls pushed together to meet,
without you our family feels incomplete.
You helped me see my experiences as gifts,
and I have learned to live with monsters,
to coexist.
I will forever crave sushi and the LA nightlife,
thank you for loving me and sharing your life.

Life Gets Better

The opaque clouds will soon blow over,
revealing the beautiful blue sky above them.

KERRI LINK

Meaning Through My Mother's Eyes

Conflict arises the minute humans
learn how to communicate.
We try to make sense of each other,
but how do we process and interpret the
meaning in someone else's thoughts or words?
Always assigning meaning to all we observe,
we communicate and analyze until we succeed or
fail, hopefully working through the conflict.
We will always have different interpretations,
but can learn to agree that we are different.
And as long as we understand that fact,
we can accept that we view experience uniquely.
To communicate, we reduce uncertainty,
which is critical in the hope of resolution,
as well as maintaining our relationships.
Do we actually get closer
to understanding each other?
I think we do.

I Miss You

It's so quiet without you here.

I hope you know I live in fear.

Fear that, one day, I will not remember you.

We will meet again in heaven.

That is one thing the world cannot undo.

Stand For Something

Freedom isn't free.
Someone fought for our freedom.
They sacrificed their life
so we could feel safe, be safe.
We are all fighting for something.
I will be forever grateful to those
who fought for our country.

I Won't Change My Values For You

You killed the vibe,

and everything began to fade.

I wanted to believe our love was real.

You wanted more, and I couldn't ignore

that you swore to love me,

but wanted to explore.

I could no longer allow

the double life you led.

Wanting others to come into our space

was disrespectful to our marriage.

Had I followed your lead,

it would have destroyed me.

I had to make a choice to stay or leave.

Choosing against you wasn't easy.

It was the lifestyle you chose that ruined us.

My children will one day see that I fought for

them.

Illusion vs Delusion

I dreamed of a beautiful life by your side.

I trusted your thoughts and ideas.

I believed in you, I fought for you.

I loved you, but you were delusional.

You chose to see the worst in people,

and for a while I believed your view.

But they were lies you brought into our home,

and you spewed them into the air we breathed.

I'm sorry you chose to live in a space

where I could no longer inhale the fear and

hatred you were consumed by.

Now I know the difference; it was all an illusion.

Summer Daze

Pregnant in the heat of summer.
After so many miscarriages
I was mentally exhausted.
You wanted to live your life without any changes,
but having children changes everything.
I didn't know we were living in your world,
where only you existed.
I tried to live there for years,
realizing we weren't going in the same direction.
You didn't know love, you were so twisted.
Sad, you created a world where only you could
exist.
I am moving on and no longer in your daze.

We Will Always Survive

You took it out on a 17-year-old girl.

For that I will never be able to forgive you.

A young, kind soul,

she loved you like a father.

She has learned to thrive without you too.

Indescribable, what you have caused.

You tried destroying everything

and everyone in your path.

Well, we survived.

We will always survive.

Hiding in Plain Sight

I no longer want to feel intense shame,

the type of shame I felt when I was with you.

The self-blame and grief I've endured.

You tried to publicly humiliate me,

introducing me to a dark side of life

I never knew existed.

So instead of living, I became withdrawn.

No longer would I take your abuse.

I wasn't the crazy one.

You were a bottom feeder,

the worst kind of manipulator.

I couldn't live in your satanic presence any longer.

It took me years to see, but you were only

humiliating yourself.

Now I'm free.

Remembering What I Value

I will spend the next years

recollecting my values

and choosing what is right for me

and what isn't.

I have a moral compass

that means something to me.

Why did I choose to sweep my worth away?

To make you happy?

You have no respect for me.

You never did.

You Tore People Down

You tore people down,
only to build them into something you desired.
You manufactured little followers
so you could rule them in your little world.
You wanted to take charge of everyone and
everything,
Molding them into your likeness.

Nobody has the right to destroy a soul,
to strip them of their God-given gifts.
Nobody should abuse that power,
eradicate what you see as weak.

You are the challenged one.
Everyone has the right to be free.
Free from those who try to dominate and control.

I Don't Need your Permission

You told me I couldn't walk
across the street without you.
Watch me! I shouted,
as I skipped to the other side.
I don't need anything from you.
I never have, and I never will.
Not ever.
I give myself permission to live my life,
no longer living in fear
of your abuse and anger.
You betrayed us all.
I give myself permission to heal.
Maybe by understanding
the role of a narcissist,
we will be able to clearly see
that we deserve to know love and forgiveness.
I give myself permission to forgive.
You tried destroying all of our lives.
Instead, you ruined your own.
Sadly, you chose to work hard
at destroying anything good.
I'm sorry that you didn't fight for us

but against us.

I now give myself permission to let you go.

Color of a Kiss

Were you the one who was meant to draw me in?

Draw me in red and gold.

What is the color of your kiss?

Gold sequins dripping in red blood.

I'm dying inside.

What am I made of?

I gave you my soul.

You took my heart.

What is the color of your kiss?

Gold sequins dripping in red blood.

You were the fire within me,

but you chose to steal my kiss.

I am whole without you.

Red and gold will never be the same.

What is the color of your kiss?

Gold sequins dripping in red blood.

I no longer care.

I am worthy without your kiss.

Freedom From The Past

When you think of shattered dreams,
I hope you think about all the women you've hurt,
and how we survived the trauma and drama
while you were left with nothing but your fate.
I thought our life was heaven-made,
but once I knew there were other women,
that love began to fade.

Now I'm free.
No more you.
It's only me.
And that's the way I want it to be.
The only way it can be.
Now I'm free.
No more you.
It's only me.
And that's the only way to be free.

How could I have been so blind?
I never thought I would find a love like ours.
I wanted you, but you needed more than me.
Thank God I saw a brighter path.

It wouldn't take my lifetime to figure out the math.

It was me who needed more.

No longer would you use me like you had before.

You actually became such a bore.

Now I'm free.

No more you.

It's only me.

That's the way it was meant to be.

Now I'm free.

No more you.

It's only me.

And that's the only way.

I was ever going to be free.

For I was meant to be loved and adored.

Not something you viewed as another award.

I've moved on and made my peace.

I've found my power,

and all the abuse I shall release.

Because I'm free.

No more you, it's only me.

The only way for me to be free.

You Were Consistent at Lying

If someone hadn't told me
for the thirtieth time
that you were unfaithful,
that you had cheated on me from the start,
would we still be together,
living in your deceit?

Marriage Wasn't For You

I never wanted more than you.
We were happy for so many years,
but you were always running.

Running to hunt more.
...work more
...sex more.

While I was just surviving,
raising our children
with you gone all the time.
I was just existing as a single parent.

You should have never married me.
You took a beautiful experience away from me.
You were never going to be faithful to
anyone but yourself.

Pain In These Trees

I met your face in these trees.
I fell in love with you in these trees.

We built a family and a life in these trees.
You grew family businesses in these trees.

I'm teaching the children forgiveness.
All of this hate has caused nothing but illness.

Yet I see the family name daily, regardless.
On buildings and jerky, on billboards and cars.

I look above these trees at the beautiful stars,
remembering we have memories in these trees.

We built a life together in these trees.
You proposed to me in these trees.

But our love was destroyed in these trees.
As was as an entire family that lived in these trees.

For generations.

Small Towns

Did people move to this small town
because they committed a crime?
This would be a perfect hideout
if you were in a witness protection program.
Nobody would ever find you.
Nobody will find me here either.

Living In My Closet to Survive

I lived in fear of crowded places.
Being a princess in my closet
didn't require seeing other faces.
I was hiding from the monsters of traumatic abuse,
but one day I decided to get help, not another
excuse.
The monsters don't live inside my mind any
longer,
a team of angels now teaches me how to be
stronger.
I still remember that closet, the one that saved me.
I will continue to live in the present, not the past,
for I have set the monsters free.

Will I Disappear?

Will I disappear?
I can't keep it hidden,
but I can fly
into the darkness of the night.
Nobody knows I am above the trees.
Until now, I could hide high in the night sky,
watching life beneath me.
Will I disappear into the dark abyss?
Will I even be missed?

I Can't Hear You

Don't raise your voice to me.

I'm not your possession,

I was born to run free.

Never again will I respond to such volume.

You're just a pathetic clown,

trapped in a heavily faded costume.

I'm Leaving

I'm leaving internal hell,
a continuing practice on my journey.
I'm leaving today,
this is the right time to exit.
It won't be easy.
I believed this was life,
but it isn't,
so it is time to exit

My marriage,
negative environments,
self-doubt,
unhealthy relationships,
medicine that numbed me,
living daily inside trauma and pain,
the safety of residing in a space
that is no longer needed,
my obsession with food,
saying yes to everything,
not having boundaries,
listening to the negative voice in my head,
living as others suggest,

sacrificing my happiness.

These ideas and ways of living no longer serve me.
I will no longer relinquish control of my life.
I will live mindful of what I need to do
for myself
so I can live the best life that I was meant to create,
no longer living in fear and chaos.

So watch as I exit hell,
no longer allowing gravity to suck me in.
I choose to instead rise, knowing
that I will be who God created me to be,
and then I will reintroduce myself.

2009

A year to forget.

It was a year of regrets.

My marriage was a lie.

I filed for divorce

when I saw he wouldn't change.

My favorite aunt died of cancer,

and I wasn't sure my mom would survive.

Kaila graduated and could leave this mess,

but I wasn't ready for her to move away.

Neither was her little sister, Kenia.

Keira was very sick that year.

I wasn't sure she would be ok.

The boys were barely two.

How would I make it on my own?

Where would we live?

Would we be okay?

Would he ruin my relationship with each of you?

I would need my team to pull me through.

This actual nightmare

was trying to kill me, silently.

If Memory Serves Me Correctly

The only one your memory served was you.
You
self-righteous
narcissistic
pig.

It's 2024.
I've been sitting in a courtroom
listening to your lies since 2006.

Don't you ever tire of telling lies?
Never answering the attorney's questions?
Never having an answer for the judge?
You have wasted so much of my time.
Only a few more years.

My memory serves me well.
I know every lie you told.
And you lied under oath.
My memory has taught me many lessons.

The best was leaving you.

N Stands For Noble, Not Narcissist

I understand some live too close to a narcissist.

I just ask that you grow to know

right from wrong,

good from evil.

And I pray you choose to be noble.

Someone to be admired and respected,

instead of someone who wants to

be admired and lacks empathy, a narcissist.

What They Need

Why did I marry someone...

Someone who would take joy...

Joy in destroying me?

I want to know why.

Why do you continue to manipulate?

Manipulate the precious souls we created?

Created out of love?

Love doesn't destroy...

Destroy people you love...

Love is what they need.

What Is the Job of a Judge?

Why do you stand by,
allowing the manipulator to win?
It is the kids who lose in the end,
because you failed to do your job.
Why don't we focus on the kids?
You'd rather protect the criminal.
You shaped and bent the rules
for the abuser.
Was your interpretation honest or fair?
Without prejudice?
It wasn't.
Maybe someone should
keep eyes on you.

Divorce Won't Define Me

Fighting for what is right isn't wrong.

Freedom can be expensive.

I have been in court for twenty years.

Most people can't afford to be in court that long.

How is that fair?

The judicial system only works for wealthy men.

Even if you are a woman who can afford to win,

you won't.

Your kids won't.

Who controls what the attorneys and judges do?

The mistakes (some intentional) they make?

It's Hard to Prove Harassment

Why do some people live to harass others?

Did I not play into your hand?

Go along with what you demanded of me?

Sorry, did I insult your intelligence

while you were seeking attention

and trying to gain power by humiliating me?

Did I make you feel less than you are?

Were you trying to gain superiority?

Is that why you bully people

and harass others?

To make us feel little, small, non-existent,

uncomfortable?

Your threatening demeanor,

intimidation, ridicule,

mockery, insults, put-downs.

It must have surprised you that I walked away.

You have zero control over me.

You no longer affect me in any way.

Change a Courtroom for the Abused

The first experience victims have

while walking into a courtroom

is one of hope and triumph.

Feeling confident in the *system,*

believing the judge will follow the laws.

During the following days,

you enter the room trying not to deflate,

even though you see clearly

that he's ruling in your spouse's favor.

You remain hopeful,

but the patterns are forming.

The judge views you as a threat

to a man's world and his money.

And you realize he won't be ruling in your favor.

The outcome of a courtroom experience

for a victim can't be determined by

a judge when he can't be fair, unbiased.

Remember to go into a courthouse

with eyes wide open.

Remain optimistic.

But know that you never can assume what the

outcome will be.

Fighting for Life

You were fighting for your life.
You still are, all these years later.
I fought for you for so many years.
I fought for us—you, me, the kids.
I believed in you, but you were lost,
fighting for power and money
when you should have been fighting for us.
I found my way back to survival mode
and remained there for years,
protecting our children from
what I believed was the enemy.
I was stripped of my values during those years,
giving everything I had to raise you high
so you wouldn't die.
We needed you to find your way back,
but you are still lost.
Sometimes I can't even believe
you are still in this fight,
a fight that tried to kill us all.
Even so, I know who I am today.
Never again will I doubt my value.
I will remain strong and fight for life.

Bullets for You

I am remembering all the lies and pain
you put me through.
When did I realize I wouldn't
take another bullet for you?
I felt like another mounted animal in your
collection.
I could no longer breathe within your obsession.
The women all came forward, and instead of dying,
I surpassed you,
no longer to feel or be seen as undervalued.
Soaring to a different frequency,
one you will never be able to tap into,
was the first step in a new life.
An unbelievable breakthrough.

Checkmate

In the game of chess, the king may be worth more.
But if I had invented the game,
the queen would have had equal value.
Although you viewed me as a pawn, I wasn't.
And you most certainly were never a king.
Not in a chess game.
Nor in real life.

Life in the Present

All that matters in life
while deconstructing
negative belief systems
that keep us from growing
is that you have a
supportive team of warriors
who all stand together,
new ideas unfolding.

Friends With Benefits

What a horrible thing for people
to casually throw in your face.

So, are you friends with benefits?
Huh? Well are you?

Maybe Alanis Morissette
started this phrase in the '90s
with the song "Head over Feet".

"You're my best friend, best friend with benefits."

There are blogs with the rules of FWB,
so remember, if you see me with someone,
don't ask me if we are FWB.
Because it's none of your business.

In return, I will give you the *benefit* of the doubt
that you aren't an a**hole.

False Narratives

No longer will I do things at my own expense.

I won't be disrespected or underestimated.

No amount of money

will pay for what I have endured.

I dare you to do it better than I have.

I value my contribution to this family.

I invested in this family for years.

That is worth something.

Everything.

I am reframing my storylines

and I won't apologize.

I'm making room for my future.

My magic is just beginning to unfold.

Say Yes to Opportunity

There are opportunities all around us.
Be open to them.
Wake up from the Land of Nod.
Take a chance.
Take a risk.
My first step was getting off medication.
It had numbed me, which I wanted.
The next step was reaching out for help.
Moving out of comfort and into mystery.
From old ways to new ways of thinking.
I am mentally healthy.
I have learned so much.
I'm happier now because I choose to be.
I am the brightest version of myself.
Until tomorrow.
Then I will shine even brighter.
I am diving into my creativity,
in love with my new life.
I know what I was made for.
And what all the lovely people who
come and go were made for.
This is my time.

I'm Limitless

Everything we do in life
comes in divine timing.

The final years of my life
will be focused on others.

On this journey,
I've been researching,
so as to help others.

Sometimes I will share light,
and sometimes darkness,
for I have experienced both sides.

I am now in a place of recognition.
I know who I am.

I believe that helping others heal
is part of why we're here.

We are limitless.

The Lake Is My Mirror

I see a life worth living
as I listen and hear God's voice.
This might be the most beautiful place on Earth.

When the world grows dim around me,
I close my eyes and see even clearer
what I truly desire.

I have changed my world.
The lake mirrors how to truly live.
Looking at the lake, I see everything.

My Evolution

I can look back,
but I won't return.
I hesitate at the thought of losing ground,
but I'm unwilling to backslide.
I see instead an evolution.

My evolution.

I am evolving in my identity.
I am moving on,
never to remain stuck in the snapshot,
living moment to moment.
Constantly transforming and changing.

I Dare You

I dare you to dream and try new things.
I dare you to fight for your future
and make positive changes.
I dare you to be truthful
and persistent in all that matters.
I dare you to be kind to yourself
and others.
I dare you to be tolerant
and have patience.
I dare you to follow your intuition
and believe in yourself.

Nobody said it would be easy, but
I dare you to live the best life
only you can live.

I Won't Dim My Light

I am a young poet,
even though I may be old.

I lived in the dark and didn't know
I could discover new meaning.

What once felt sorrowful
has become my greatest desire.

I now describe what I know
and what I am learning.

No longer will I dim my light.

KERRI LINK

If I Could Bottle an Experience

I'll be okay,

but never in every way.

Please see me as more

than what happened to me.

It's hard to hide

with all the build-up inside.

I need to be free.

I can't wait any longer to be me.

I don't want to bottle my feelings.

My voice can no longer hold

what needs to come out of me.

Life As It Should Be

Isn't it ironic
that life is magical
...and yet I didn't recognize it?
Wanting to forever soar like an eagle
but not knowing how to fly,
never knowing I could live in the middle
...and be okay in the struggle.
Less anxiety and depression,
no drugs to numb the pain,
I learned to sit in my thoughts and listen.
Away from the noise,
...so much noise.
And I am no longer her,
but I am a new her,
climbing beautiful mountains,
capable of flying like the eagle,
learning to live like I never knew I could.

I am free.

Special Gifts Along the Way

You gave me the tools to freedom.

I clenched onto every word for life.

Until you, I didn't know there was a better way.

You showed me proof that there was.

I now feel powerful.

I now know I am worthy.

I no longer have to live in a place of punishment.

I was not the one at fault.

I was the victim.

I have lived in that dark space long enough.

I want you to know that you have been my

North Star.

I will be forever grateful for you,

Julie Harper.

I will never forget the safe space you created for

me.

You gave me wings to fly,

wings to discover a new way of life.

I am free.

What Is the Point?

The point is, I want to live.

I have so much I want to do.

I have so much I want to learn.

I am excited about everything.

I won't let depression

or panic attacks

steal my joy.

Anxiety will not control my life.

I am learning to rise above it all,

and when something tries to creep in,

I have the tools to remain free.

I am free.

No Longer Stuck

I was stuck in time,

only finding comfort

in the weakness and pain

of other women.

I didn't want to grieve any longer.

I have chosen to use my wings to fly.

I am free.

Can You See Me Now?

No longer will I hide in the shadows.
No longer will I carry so much shame.

No longer will I be powerless.
No longer will I live in isolation.

I won't be invisible any longer.
Can you see me now?

Inspiration For All

I'm a mystery,

enjoying the game of discovery

as one of God's divine beings.

So rewarding some days,

learning to take

the exceptional with the unacceptable.

It can all shift so quickly,

knowing that life won't end there,

continuing to show up as your entire self.

Remembering that life changes,

furnishes us with advantages and disadvantages,

strengths and weaknesses.

Keep moving forward,

transforming with all I acquire,

everything in life is a teacher.

Be open to breaking through,

extend as far as you can into this process,

be the world's inspiration.

Voice As Big As the Sea

I am the hero in my story,

my voice is as big as the sea.

I was kidnapped.

I was raped.

But they were unable to take my life.

I got away

...and I am free.

I will use my voice to help others,

so they can be the hero in their own stories.

Creating Distance

You can't erase me as an individual;
I'm a force.

I can't even pick a lane I'm so unique.

I could never have fit into your world;
my story is too powerful.

I'm moving on,
and I won't be looking back.

UNTIL NOW

The Door That Leads to More

Using pain as positive energy
is the way to so much more,
guiding me down a path
I have never walked before.

Pain as a door
that enhances my existence
will help guide me and
give me strength to go the distance.

Seeing pain as a gift
makes me a survivor, not a victim.
This will become
quite a power shift in wisdom.

Walking in courage
through that door you will see,
pain used as positive energy
teaches us to live free.

Time For a Power Shift

The day that I stopped giving my power away,
what an amazing feeling that was.
Taking back the control that was always mine.
I was labeling myself; it was nothing but lies.
The truth is, I am capable of great things.

Words Bring Peace

Writing poetry in the sunshine
has become my happy place.
It has proven to be a healing space.

How the Mind Protects Us

For years I couldn't deal with my abduction.
Don't you find it peculiar?

I was kidnapped and raped.
They were going to kill me.

Why was I unable to discuss that?

Unable to cope with the truth,
I would spend years saying I was fine.

I find it fascinating
that my mind protected me.

Kept my secret hidden, concealed,
so I couldn't be hurt again.

Then a doctor helped me deal with the nightmares
and gave me tools to live with my trauma.

Grateful to you, Dr. Krall.

That Was Then, This Is Now

Until now,
I didn't want to feel.
I wanted to die, to leave this place.

Then I realized,
my life is worth living.
I am ready to feel all emotion.

That is what living is.
I am ready to feel it all.
I acknowledge every high and every low.

I am marching toward life,
not away from it.
Having a life to live is a gift.

I choose to grow with the good and the bad.

Strength Runs Deep

How many battles do we have to
endure before finding peace?

The fights will continue
until we take our last breath.

But we must strive to find peace
in the midst of life's conflicts.

Challenge yourself to keep reaching.
There is no end to the possibilities.

We Are Never Broken

Broken bones.

Broken souls.

Broken hearts.

Broken dreams.

Broken songs.

Broken promises.

Broken confidence.

Broken people.

We sometimes feel broken, shattered, or damaged,
but it is our scars that need to be examined.

This does not mean we are beyond repair.
Injuries open us to beauty that can't be compared.

So take the word *broken* out of your vocabulary.
I will write the announcement for its obituary.

We are all beautiful, none of us broken.

Riding The Waves Of Life

I choose to ride

the waves of love,

the waves of creativity,

the waves of passion,

the waves of adventure.

When you follow your dreams,

you just may help someone

who is seeking help along the way.

Other Choices

Don't focus on the negative voices inside.

Recognize there are other choices you can make.

Some days it's difficult to continue being positive.

Remaining true to yourself is the only way.

Fear Can Be Helpful

Until now, my vision was clouded
due to fear.
Until now, I wasn't sure how to change the
narrative.
Until now, I didn't have the tools,
tools that would give me
the self-confidence to move forward.
Until now, I didn't realize that fear helps us,
helps us understand that it won't be easy,
but we need to still try.
It is the only way to move forward.
It may not be comfortable,
but the other side of fear will be better
when it works out.
And even when it doesn't,
you can decide to keep moving,
or possibly pivot.
Take action and go forward
until you find what you enjoy.
Until you find something you are good at.
I won't be held back any longer.
This is what freedom looks like to me.

Before You Get Married

Before you get married,
how will you know
without a doubt
that he will be faithful?
You won't.
You can't.
How could you?

Life Is Truly Joyful

Until now, I felt like I was living out a life
sentence.
Thanks to a new way of thinking,
I have discovered acceptance.
I'm researching my trauma and
getting the answers needed.
I'm reframing negative thoughts
and beliefs, and I've succeeded.
I can move forward, knowing that
trauma inside me can't destroy.
Because my grief has brought me back to joy.

Needing More In Life

So many statements surround me,
telling me I need to find
a REAL job in life.
Saying that just being a mom
shouldn't fulfill me.
Then there are the people
who think I am terrible
for wanting more.
For needing more.
For craving more.
In life, of life.
I won't be living in the past.
I won't feel guilty
for craving more
than motherhood alone.
There are so many things I want to do.
I love being a mother,
but I am opening the door
for the possibility of more.
Unapologetically.

Let's Go

I was told the other day
that everything before forty is research.
That makes me beyond ready.

Until Now I Have Allowed Disrespect

Loving yourself tenderly

doesn't connect with disrespect.

You deserve to be loved gently.

Why don't we understand that?

Raising our children to see us being mistreated

will continue to haunt us for generations.

Why can't we seem to change?

It takes a lot of work to break this cycle.

Some will make it out and get to the other side.

Some won't.

I am seeing a change.

We are learning from each other.

We will break the cycle together and teach love,

instilling new ways of caring for others,

everywhere around us.

The Flower of Hope

Fields of poppies
stretching out to meet the sun.
Can you visualize the brilliant blooms?
Feel the warmth of the light?
Hear the whirling rush of wind
while recalling the scent of summer?
I begin to experience the taste of hope.

Shining Bright for Me

Until now, I was frozen.

I didn't know how to move forward.

Thank you, God, for shining a light.

A light back to you.

So I could find the true me.

And shine my light forever.

Shining Too Bright

Am I too much for you?
I won't ever apologize for it.
Because this is who I am.
I love to sparkle.
Glow, even.
Please let this be your reason to see
that you, too, are unique, and
we all have the right to shine bright.

We All Have a Story

Until now, I didn't know
anyone would ever know my story.
I didn't think anyone would care.
Putting pain into words
has been a tool that saved me.

Writing Burns In My Soul

While writing a memoir, I felt heavy,
as if the experiences were on my back.
So I decided to express my thoughts
in an unfamiliar way, and
I found that poetry began to fuel
something new, deep inside of me
that I had never experienced before.

Magnetic Experiences

Some days, I am on overload.
How do you help others with grief
when you have not dealt with your own?
I am learning to face things that trigger me,
trying to understand what it all means.
Now that I am beginning to unmask
things that have tormented me,
I will better be able to understand others'
suffering.

I Have a Name

I am someone.

I am qualified.

I am special.

I am love.

I am strong.

I am creative.

I am awake.

I am curious.

I am seeking.

I am grateful.

I am motivated.

I am complex.

I am smart.

I am hopeful.

I am inspired.

I am joyful.

I am honest.

I am alive.

As I am.

Speak Louder Please

Then I heard a faint echo,
the echo of so many who tried whispering
wisdom into my soul.
Words that could have saved me
from years of self-torture.
But I couldn't hear your wisdom.
Until now, I was submerged in murky water,
and couldn't understand the words you
whispered so softly.
I had to rise out of that gloomy water
to meet your words.
So I reached up to the light,
pulling myself out of the darkness.
Now I bloom like the lotus flower.
I can hear you.
I am forever grateful.

Endings and Beginnings

Situations in life can have
hundreds of different endings.

Endings force us to move
toward new beginnings.

You can't always predict
how something will end.

A marriage.
A pregnancy.
A job.
A painting.
A friendship.
A life.

It rarely turns out the way you visualized,
but there will be times when your journey
will end better than you ever dreamed.

Giving Back

I choose to serve my purpose,
not my weakness.

Ebb and Flow

The ebb and flow of life is very much alive.
It somehow puts my mind into overdrive.

We learn to develop, then sustain.
Even when life drags us through undesired pain.

Actually, ebb and flow is about mental peace.
All anxiety varies and changes, then will cease.

The changes in our lives and relationships
will connect us with life-lasting companionships.

When I Arrive, I Will Unpack

Unpack a new sense of freedom.
It's all in what we choose to visualize,
so I choose to unpack my greatest joys.
I want this new place to be special,
so you and I can be who we are meant to be.
I will unpack my good memories,
the ones that feel, sound, smell, and taste amazing.
I won't allow myself to dwell in the pain.
I will keep those memories packed for now.
It's time to experience lighter and brighter times,
life with intense vividness.
Let's illuminate with clarity.
Nothing can dull your sparkle now.
Only your memory, if you allow.

Places That Make Us Feel More

The mountains in Sedona.

The sound of the ocean.

Driving down snowy roads with twinkling
Christmas lights.

Enfolded in the arms of a friend.

Being with my children.

Snuggled in bed with a book.

Walking my dog on a summer evening.

Crossing the finish line of a marathon.

Writing a book.

Seeing my grandchildren, picking flowers, listening
to music.

What Makes Your Senses Come Alive?

Bookstores are the buildings
I most enjoy entering.
If I see one, I must step inside.
I walk over to the nonfiction section
and gently pull out a book.
Study the design of the cover.
Glance at the author.
Smell the pages.
Read the words out loud
while trying to comprehend
what the author wants me to absorb.
Am I familiar with the author?
When did she write it?
Did she self-publish?
I sit on the floor and continue
down the rows of books until
I have touched, smelled, heard
the sound of the pages turning
and looked at each one.
I am full.

Living a Life in Words

Words make starting the day
exciting for me.
Everything I do during the day
is surrounded by words.
Listening to my favorite music
and singing along.
Putting thoughts and ideas
into my morning pages journal.
Reading the latest memoirs,
finding the right words through
writing poetry to heal,
as well as sharing conversations
with everyone I love.

Things that Glow

Fireflies, the moon, and jellyfish
all shine bright in different ways.
Let's all create a bright light,
blazing a vivid path in life with praise,
creating firelight for all to see.
Finding that magic inside us
will set us all free.

Slow and Steady

Like a maple tree
blowing in the breeze,
musical are the leaves.
Veins radiating out like a star,
roots deep within the ground.
Leaves change into autumn shades
of red, yellow, and orange,
then turn brown and fall to the ground.
In the spring, they bud and
burst back to life.
They produce syrup, but
take their time by design.
Free to be and free to change,
taking time to grow and shine.
Something new always emerging.
This is the pulse of life.

In, Then Out

Breathe in tranquility.
Exhale suffering.

Breathe in peace.
Exhale anguish.

We Are Worthy

I see my life with new perspective,
from a wiser place.
I have reopened wounds
so that they will heal correctly this time.
I have found stability
and made peace with my past.
PTSD can sneak up on you
at any moment,
but you become better at seeing
the trauma for what it is.
You are no longer disconnected,
but instead connected to the deeper part of you
that will help you deal with other heartbreak in
life.
By giving yourself permission
to re-examine your life,
you're no longer stuck in the moment.
You become less vulnerable and more in control,
making it easier to live day to day in peace.
You are worth fighting for.

What Is Being Alone?

Is it not having a partner?
Is it when your kids move out
and your parents are gone
and you're not sure
where you will end up in the world?
Or what you will do
when your home is empty?

Maybe it's having time for yourself,
picking flowers with sun on your face,
listening to music you enjoy
while you read a new book.
Maybe it's finally living your dreams
and being able to write poetry for your soul.

KERRI LINK

Alone Doesn't Have to Mean Lonely

Until now, I felt alone.
It takes time and courage
to recognize that being alone
can be magical.
Keep searching and you will see.
Let's find our way and go forward.
To explore our passions and desires.
To discover the people and places we crave.
Our world changes daily, but we are alive.
Please choose life and live it,
no matter what that looks like.
We are never truly alone.
We have God
and a world full of beautiful people
waiting to meet us on our journey.
But only you know what direction
will bring magic to your soul.
Sometimes it's better to go alone.

Weaving Memories

While we are here on earth,
we need to take our precious memories
and weave them into the magic of
moving forward.

How We Grow

Mental growth.
Meditating with focus.

Social growth.
Surrounding yourself with positive people.

Spiritual growth.
Surrounding yourself with other believers.

Emotional growth.
Learning new things and becoming confident.

Physical growth.
Committing to a routine and getting enough sleep.

Reading Is a Vibe

I've read so many books throughout the year,
acquiring knowledge that keeps my mind clear.

Reading keeps me positive with no exception,
viewing life through my perception.

Books teach how to break unhealthy patterns,
healing on your journey is what truly matters.

So break old patterns, learn something new,
research is the way to a healthier view.

Be Soft

Soft and persistent
is how we need to be in life.
Kind to ourselves,
but always moving forward.

Trust That Your Life Is Working For You

When you believe in yourself

and all that you do,

life will work out for you.

Not always in the way you think,

but it will be the direction

that is meant for you.

Clear your mind of any negative thinking

so you can make room for healthy thoughts to

grow,

figuring out what you want and why.

Don't force things to happen,

and trust yourself;

it always works out in the end.

Visualize what you desire.

Journal your thoughts and ideas.

It will become easier once you witness

the impact that manifesting your thoughts has

on your life and those around you.

Tune into your highest frequency

and watch life change.

Manifest yourself right into happiness.

KERRI LINK

What Is Your Superpower?

I am not powerless.
You must have the wrong girl.

I chose to go my own way.
And I am limitless.

I'm unstoppable.

Life Is Full Of Promise

Until now, I looked at life as threatening.

Now I see life as an opportunity.

Life throws us difficult situations.

Healing can take a while.

I am living proof that life moves

with or without us

and that there is life after trauma.

Grandchildren Bring Joy

What ignites joy within?
It's seeing your granddaughter
for the first time.
Catching a glimpse of her smile,
hearing her voice for the first time.
Then one day, she says your name.
Watching her walk, then seeing her run.
The first Facetime on the phone when you
live in different states.
Mailing you art she created for your birthday.
First-time experiences with Charlotte
have brought me so much joy.

Pivot

I pivot when I feel restricted.

I'm driven by results.

Creating has brought me new life.

Seasons

Feel the raindrops fall from heaven with grace.

Feel the heat of sunshine on your face.

Feel the leaves crunch under your feet.

Feel the snow then press repeat.

Women In My Life

I look at the warriors around me, knowing
I can face any obstacle that comes my way.

These incredibly strong women share their stories
so others will recognize they're special one day.

Growing Tall

I choose to be the lotus flower today,
choosing to believe I am strong enough
to reach for the sun,
even when situations
try to suck me back into the murky waters.

Mondays

If you woke up this morning
wanting it to be Friday,
maybe you need a cup of coffee.

Intentional Recalibration

Wow, look out new year.
I have a new mantra.

I lived this past year envisioning.
Envisioning a new life for myself.

This new perspective on life
is becoming a new vision for the future.

The best is yet to come!

In the Present

I thought I had gone back to the numbness,
the emptiness I felt years ago.
But I realized today that people can't live
in constant joy, either.
It's normal to live in a calm state of being,
excitement and disappointments will come and go.
So find your baseline and learn to adjust,
being aware of the highs and lows.
You will find that relaxed space
will give you the mindspace to grow.

What's That Holiday in February?

Here comes Cupid again, no need to explain.

Engagement rings, chocolates, flowers, champagne.

Is this about love or is it all just insane?

It all seems to be a ludicrous campaign.

If you feel you have a connection that will remain,

I'm sorry to be cynical and leave a verbal stain.

The Choices We Make

As you glance at your reflection,
I pray you choose the right direction.

Trust Your Intuition

Have you ever been in a relationship
where you felt you made progress
then realized you never will?
Where they promised to go forward
in truth and kindness, and then they didn't?
Someone wise once told me
not to be upset when someone
allows you into their dark soul.
They are being consistent in who they are.

Trust yourself.

When They Tell You Who They Are

Are they consistent as *liars*?

Are they consistent as *manipulators*?

Are they consistently *toxic*?

Are they consistently *rotten*?

That is your sign to
break the pattern and
make better choices.

Who Is Your Tribe?

Who do you have
magic moments with?
Who energizes you?
Who sets your soul
on fire?
Make these people
your priority.

Do You Hear Me?

Deprogramming yourself, if you have the desire,
creates someone you will always admire.
To free yourself from societal submission,
you may find the world in considerable
opposition.
Yet others will find the courage to rejoice,
to live no longer fearful of having a voice.
We all have the right to freedom of speech,
I will no longer be discouraged and besieged.

I Am Going To Be Okay

I wasn't sure how
to process my past.

I chose self-destruction
to find an escape.

Lately I have felt a shift,
it has been golden.

This new freedom I have found
has regenerated creativity in me.

Keep Walking Forward

There may be a long-worn path
behind me.

But there is green grass still growing
in front of me.

Tick Tock

Is there still time for me?
Am I too old
to find my passion?
To find love?
Every day that slips away,
I feel myself chasing
everything I put on hold.
Maybe it's too late for me,
but what if it's not?

Rise

Even though we have gone
quite the distance,
there is still room for more
laws to be set in place
for all the vulnerable children.

Embedded Deep Within Our Souls

We have everything we need
to do amazing things.

We just need to keep listening.

Don't miss the miracles,
no matter how small.

Sometimes they sound
like a whisper.

The Way

Through trauma
we are handed a gift
to be able to see ourselves
on a truer, deeper level
with so much more meaning.
It's time to take
what we have discovered
in ourselves and
change the way
we live in the universe.

Love Is Everything

Love can even flow through venom.
You may be grieving, but
poison can bring momentum.
Use it as your spiritual weapon to spread
your wings
and soar high
into the heavens.

Loving You

Have I ever told you
that you are my happy place,
my healing space?
Well, now you know.

Staying In Your Own Lane

I am winning just by staying in the race.
There will be so many obstacles that I will yet face.
I will continue on my journey, remain in my lane,
with all of the highs and lows, sunshine or rain.
And when I finally cross that finish line,
I hope I am greeted by loved ones and sunshine.

Let's Join Hands

Until now, I was intimidated by people
I felt held all the power.

Today, I know I am equal to
anyone else I might encounter.

Our Story

We all have a powerful story.

Choosing to help others with your gift

is for His glory.

Don't miss out on your miracle.

It's difficult some days to reach for your pinnacle.

Follow your heart and your wonderful

imagination

on your journey of incredible transformation.

Love who you are and who you continue to

become on the inside.

And what lies next in life,

only you and the universe can decide.

I Am Finding My Place In The World

My candlelight has been dim, almost nonexistent.
Until now, I allowed people to extinguish my
flame.
Lately, that candle has been dancing
with luminosity and hope.
The closer I get to finding my place and my people,
the brighter that candle burns with brilliance.
I will continue to light my candle
until it illuminates on its own.
Because then I will have found the place I belong.

A Better Tomorrow

Every day we are building something.

A family, a home, a career.

A garden, a work of art, a dream.

We create with our minds, our hands, our words.

We add things and we take others away.

Always working toward a better life.

Who holds the paintbrush to your design?

To your masterpiece?

You do.

Striving For Better

I'm not running from ghosts anymore.
I'm running toward a brighter future.

To My Sister

Thank you for helping me see
that my life, too, has true meaning.
I've taken my trauma and discovered
that talking with you about my past
has given me a purpose in life.
And has given me courage to go forward
and want to give back to others in grief.

Worthy

Instead of feeling
shameful and unworthy,
I gave new meaning to my past,
giving me the courage
to stand up for others.

People who have been
abused in this world
should not have to go
through the rest of their lives
feeling unworthy.

Let's help reverse the way
victims perceive themselves.
We are strong, courageous, and kind,
forever worthy of shining
the brightest parts of who we are.

Brave and Inspired

Until now, I didn't think
what I had to say
was of importance.

Now I am ready to be heard.

I made it to the editor.
Most people never make
it to the editor.

Why Am I Running Toward a High?

Passion is a feeling you can't maintain.
I have been running toward passion
and finally realize it too comes and goes.
No longer will I be chasing passion,
even though I enjoy the high.
Finding balance has become my
new focus to experiencing true happiness.

KERRI LINK

Focus on Balance

I live to shine,
shine bright.

Am I dimming my light
because I choose
to walk through life single?

I dimmed my light
most of my life.

Now I can shine again.
Not because I am single,
but because
I am whole.

Life Now

I don't follow through
on most things.
Just those
that are important to me.

We Are All Different

I find that I am
not talking in circles,
and I never was.
It is how I process,
and I want to be mindful
of words I share
with others in the world.
I am protective of my words,
protective of what I am creating.

Let Me Reframe This

Books end, but life goes on.
We all have unfinished business
before we leave this place.

This book will end too,
but I intend to continue
filling the pages of my life.

Until my last breath.

I Want to Help

I am drawn to pen and paper.
I hope you are able to decipher
through my words
that it is possible
to go through hell
and come back with your story
and have a purpose.

We Are Meant To Be Free

So for now,
goodbye.
To trauma.
To abuse.
To the fear of food,
of men.
of rape,
of anxiety
and depression.
I bid you farewell.
I have other chapters
to explore,
other poems to write.
About bravery and
finding my way home.
About entering a new world
of inspiration, curiosity,
hope, and intense love.
To go forward with the desire
to inspire others to heal
and realize they too are whole.

About the Author

Kerri Link is a mother and grandmother living in the Midwest. She is happiest with a book in her hands, at a concert, or hiking in the mountains. Her love of words has finally brought her to poetry.

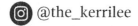 @the_kerrilee